Ingredients for Mastery

To Angela Lee Duckworth, Ph.D.
Mentor, teacher and inspiration.

How to Achieve Excellence Using Positive Psychology

Copyright © 2015, 2016 Paolo Terni

All rights reserved.

No part of this book may be reproduced in any form or by any electronic or mechanical means, including information storage and retrieval systems, without permission in writing from the author and/or publisher, except by a reviewer who may quote brief passages in review.

ISBN: 978-0-9855920-8-0

Published by Paolo Terni BriefCoachingSolutions
California, USA

Ingredients for Mastery: How to Achieve Excellence Using Positive Psychology.

Dr. Paolo Terni, MAPP

How to Achieve Excellence Using Positive Psychology

Table of Contents

MASTERY 7

Setting the stage in 5D 11
    CHAPTER ONE 13
    DIRECTION 13
    DEVOTION 17
    DEVELOPMENT 19
    DOING WHAT AND WHY 23
    DOING GOOD 27

The 10 Ds for Mastery 31
    DRILL 33
    DETERMINATION 39
    DEDICATION 43
    DIGNITY 47
    DILIGENCE 53
    DISCIPLINE 61
    DRIVE 67
    DELTA 73
    DOWNTIME 77
    DETAIL 81

Through duty to delight 85
    DELIGHT 87

    Dr. Paolo Terni, MAPP 91

How to Achieve Excellence Using Positive Psychology

MASTERY

The topic of this book is how to achieve mastery – of a craft, of a profession, of a trade, of a hobby. The fields of application range from becoming a runner to learning how to speak a foreign language; from becoming an excellent salesperson to becoming an inspirational leader; from learning how to perform as a piano soloist to learning how to code.

From this book's perspective, mastery is defined not by its end results but by its starting point. If you are operating at a professional level, what you find in this book will help you get even better. If you start from zero, what you find in this book will help you become an amateur who can impress.

Technically speaking, what you find in these pages is often referred to as the psychology of achievement, which in turn is part of one of the most popular frameworks for understanding well-being: PERMA. According to Martin Seligman, the father of positive psychology, the ingredients for a flourishing life are the following: **P**ositive emotions; full **E**ngagement with life; positive **R**elationships; **M**eaning and purpose; and **A**chievement or mastery for its own sake. These elements are summed up in the acronym: **PERMA**. <u>This book is about the letter A in PERMA.</u>

Achievement implies accomplishing something.

But reaching a desired outcome often requires more than just mastery. You might also need elements outside of your control: the right break at the right time; the right personality or physical build; the right environment; and so on and so forth.

So I went for mastery (and interchangeably, excellence). That is under your control.

Each chapter illustrates one key ingredient for achieving mastery.

All the strategies that I present in this book are grounded in specific psychology research findings, so at the end of each chapter you will find references.

To make these findings even more useful to your pursuit of mastery, I have packaged them so you can use them as single-word mantras, all beginning with the letter D. This will help you to orient yourself and to stay the course when the going gets tough.

Taken together, these chapters answer the question: how can I achieve mastery in [fill in the blanks]?

To learn more:

Seligman, M. E. P. (2011). *Flourish: A visionary new understanding of happiness and wellbeing.* New York: Free Press.

Ingredients for Mastery

Setting the stage in 5D

Ingredients for Mastery

CHAPTER ONE
DIRECTION

Choose to master something that is meaningful to YOU...

di·rec·tion
 Noun: direction; plural noun: directions
 - a general way in which someone or something is developing.
 "New directions in painting and architecture".
 Synonyms: orientation, inclination, leaning, tendency, bent, and preference.

Before throwing yourself in the pursuit of mastery, ask yourself one question: do you want it?

The emphasis is on *you*, and the emphasis is on *want*.

It should not be what your partner wants you to excel at, but what <u>you</u> want to excel at.

It should not be the skill that you think you should master, but the skill that you <u>want</u> to master.

In other words, are you pursuing mastery in [fill in the blank], because:

a) It would bring you a sense of meaning and purpose in your life;

b) It would bring you social approval, money, power and fame.

If you chose option (b), you might want to re-label your pursuit.

Psychologists talk about the importance of developing skills that matter to you by using different "constructs" (a technical term for concepts that are measured via scales and questionnaires):

- **Intrinsic motivation.** You are intrinsically motivated if you are interested in getting better at something for its own sake. On the other hand, you are extrinsically motivated if you do something as a means to an end. For example, you might be learning all that there is to learn about the American Civil War because you are a history buff and you love the subject (intrinsically motivated); or you might be learning about the American Civil War because you have a test or because you need that job at the museum (extrinsically motivated).

- **Self-concordant goals.** You have self-concordant goals if they match your personality and your potential. If you are 6 foot 4, athletic and interested in sports, then pursuing excellence in basketball sounds like a good idea. Or maybe you are the life of the party and you are not interested at all in contemplative practices. In that case, choosing to master the art of ancient Japanese flower arrangement (Ikebana) might be therapeutic and might bring balance to your personality, but it is not a self-concordant goal.

Ingredients for Mastery

- **Harmonious passions**. Your passions are harmonious if they find expression in freely chosen activities that support harmonious growth, whereas they are obsessive if they translate into activities done to please others or to achieve a certain status. So, for example, if I choose to become a chess master because I want it, and my chess activities are an opportunity for me to make more friends and lead a richer life, then my passion for chess is harmonious. On the other hand, if I choose to become a chess master because I want to become famous, and I abandon all social life to retreat in the basement to study chess 24/7, then my passion qualifies as an obsession.

It turns out that if you are intrinsically motivated <u>and</u> your passion is well-integrated in your life <u>and</u> it matches who you are, then you are more likely to achieve your goals <u>while at the same time boosting your well-being</u>.

Note that finding out what matters to a person is a process that varies greatly among individuals.

For some people it is not about finding out, but about responding to a deep calling. They always knew and they feel they have no choice.

For some other people, it is about experimenting, as their interests take shape over time. It is a conscious process of trial and error, of slowly zeroing in.

For yet some others, it is an accidental discovery. They did not have a clearly defined passion, nor were they trying to find one. But then one day they try, say, an acting class or writing code and bam! They are hooked.

Finally, for some people it is not about finding out what matters to them but about what the situation is demanding of them. Something happens, an accident or an illness, and that changes everything. They found a cause, something to serve, and that gives them purpose in life.

Regardless of the process, the important thing is to be clear about why you want to become a master at [fill in the blank].

The takeaway: pursue mastery in something that matters to you.

To learn more:
Brooks, D. (2015). *The road to character.* New York: Random House.

Ryan, R. M., & Deci, E. L. (2000). Self-determination theory and the facilitation of intrinsic motivation, social development, and well-being. *American Psychologist, 55*(1), 68-78.

Sheldon, K. M., & Elliot, A. J. (1999). Goal striving, need-satisfaction, and longitudinal well-being: The self-concordance model. *Journal of Personality and Social Psychology, 76,* 482-497.

Vallerand, R. J., Blanchard, C., Mageau, G. A., Koestner, R., Ratelle, C., Léonard, M., ... & Marsolais, J. (2003). Les passions de l'ame: on obsessive and harmonious passion. *Journal of Personality and Social Psychology, 85*(4), 756-767.

CHAPTER TWO

DEVOTION

... Even though it is not about YOU

de·vo·tion
   Noun: devotion
   - Love, loyalty, or enthusiasm for a person, activity, or cause.
   "Elizabeth's devotion to her partner".
   Synonyms: loyalty, commitment, constancy, and allegiance.

In the previous chapter I argued that mastery in any field is such an arduous pursuit that it can be sustained only if the end goal matters to you, personally and deeply. However, here is the paradox: what you choose to do must be important to you; but once you commit, it is no longer about you — it is about the craft you are going to serve.

Mastery of a craft requires first submission to its nature.
If, for example, you want to excel at chess, you need to conform yourself to the demands of the practice of chess.
You need to understand its logic, and even more importantly, you need to participate in

chess tournaments, in chess culture, in chess institutions.

You are serving the craft of chess and its advancement.

You are belonging to a tradition that transcends you, that will transform you and that will survive you.

If, for example, you want to excel at writing, you need to devote yourself to writing.

It is no longer about what you want to do, but about what the art of writing is demanding of you.

The milestones in the pursuit of excellence are as follows:

1) You approach the path to mastery from the inside out, by first figuring out which craft matters to you (see previous chapter).

2) You pursue mastery by having the practice of the craft change you from the outside in.

3) You achieve mastery when your work starts shaping the craft.

The takeaway: The outcome of mastery is feeling in control when performing. But the process to achieve mastery requires humble submission to the service of the chosen craft.

To learn more:
Crawford, M.B. (2009). *Shop class as soulcraft: An inquiry into the value of work.* New York: Penguin.

Ingredients for Mastery

CHAPTER THREE
DEVELOPMENT

Mastery goals vs. performance goals

de·vel·op·ment
  Noun: development
  - The process of developing or being developed.
  "She traces the development of the novel".
  Synonyms: evolution, growth, maturation, expansion, spread, and progress.

Once you are clear about why you want to pursue mastery in a certain field, you need to choose the right kind of goal. You do that by stating what you want to achieve in a way that supports your striving for excellence.

In psychological literature, this kind of goal is called a **mastery goal**. A mastery goal is about getting better rather than performing well. Your yardstick is going to be progress, not achievement, at least not yet.

For example, a mastery goal could be: "to get better at chemistry", whereas a performance goal could be "to get an A in chemistry"; a mastery goal could be "getting better at sales", whereas a performance goal could be "selling 50 new policies per month". A mastery goal is about running a little bit faster or longer each week, rather than achieving a certain time; it is about eating a little bit less or better, rather than losing 20 pounds.

The opposite of mastery goals are **performance goals**. They specify an outcome (e.g., playing in an orchestra; getting a promotion) and they can be very motivating in the right context. Performance goals are "be good" goals, because achieving those goals demonstrates that you are capable and talented: you've got it.

However, in the context of the pursuit of mastery, you have not yet developed your ability to perform at a level of excellence. You are still learning, and setting a performance goal too soon might turn out to be counterproductive to your progress.

For example, suppose I want to master the art of selling.

I set for myself the performance goal of closing 15 sales per week. As Friday afternoon approaches and I am still stuck at 12 sales, I start worrying about making my goal. So I call up old customers that I think are an "easy sell", and I also ask my network for solid prospects. I end up achieving my goal and I close the week with 15 sales, but it is very unlikely that I learned anything new regarding selling.

Now imagine the same scenario, except that I have the goal of getting better each week. As Friday afternoon approaches, instead of going for

Ingredients for Mastery

slam dunks, I ask my colleagues for the hardest prospects they've had to deal with, unsuccessfully, in the past few weeks, and I give it a try. I end up making just one additional sale, and I close the week at 13 total. However, chances are that I learned more from that single difficult sale on Friday (and from all the other rejections that day) than if I had called established clients just to meet my quota.

In another example, suppose I want to become a runner.

My performance goal might be to run a marathon or to achieve a 9 minute / mile pace.

Those goals can be intimidating if I start from zero.

I might go for my first run, and discover that it takes me 10 minutes to go for less than half a mile; I go for a second run and it is a little bit better, but still way off target. Disappointed, I might give up.

But suppose instead that I set first my goal as to just get better, defined as increasing the number of minutes I run per week.

That is easy to accomplish, all I need to do is to run one more minute this week than I did last week.

Once minutes become hours and yards become miles, I can switch to a performance goal.

So, at first choose mastery goals. Focus on small progress over performance. Focus on learning instead of external validation.

Are you improving? Are you making progress? Are you learning? Do you have a better grasp of the foundations of that field?

If you choose mastery goals, you will enjoy the journey, and you will persist despite disappointments. Because occasional failures are not interruptions in your pursuit of mastery; they are the process of achieving mastery.

The takeaway: to achieve mastery, at first focus on progress instead of achievement.

To learn more:
Halvorson, H. G. (2010). *Succeed: How we can reach our goals.* New York: Penguin.

CHAPTER FOUR

DOING WHAT AND WHY

Language for increasing motivation and language for beating procrastination

do
  Verb
  Gerund or present participle: doing
  - Perform (a particular task).
  "Dad always did the cooking on Sundays".
  Synonyms: carry out, undertake, discharge, execute, perform, and accomplish.

So what do you do when you clean your house?
No, I am not interested in cleaning tips.
What I mean is, how do you think of it?

For example, would you describe cleaning the house as vacuuming and then mopping the floor; or would you describe it as making the house more comfortable for your dinner guests?

The former is **"what" thinking** — you are describing the actions that you are performing.
The latter is **"why" thinking** — you are describing why you are performing the actions.

"What" thinking is great for complex tasks that feel overwhelming. For example, mastering statistics. Break it down. What would be the first "what" step? It could be to do some research online about useful resources for beginners. That sounds doable. Do that, then move on to the next small step. Little by little, you will be on your path to mastery.

As you might have guessed, "what" thinking is also great for dealing with procrastination. Sorting out the boxes that are still in the garage two years after you moved in feels like an insurmountable task? Think in terms of "what". What is the first small thing that you need to do? It might simply be to take the box on top of the pile and sort out its contents. That sounds doable, much more doable than "organizing the mess in the garage". With "what" thinking, you'll be doing it before you'll know it.

On the other hand, "why" thinking is great for motivation.

Why are you doing it?

What is the purpose behind the specific action you are taking?

This kind of thinking is going to be invaluable in your pursuit of mastery.

Suppose I want to master a foreign language before taking a trip overseas. Here is how the two different kinds of thinking play out when you consider the upcoming practice session.

"What" thinking: I am going to listen to this tape again.

"Why" thinking: I am learning how to communicate with people from a different culture, and ultimately I am making a difference, however small, in cross-cultural relations.

Here is another example: I want to master leadership skills and I signed up for a workshop on the topic.
"What" thinking: I am going to walk in that classroom this morning to take this three-day course on leadership skills.
"Why" thinking: I am going to become the best leader I can be, so I can serve my team members and all the stakeholders even better.
Which one is more motivating?

The takeaway: beat procrastination with "what" thinking, keep motivated with "why" thinking.

To learn more:
Halvorson, H. G. (2010). *Succeed: How we can reach our goals.* New York: Penguin.

How to Achieve Excellence Using Positive Psychology

CHAPTER FIVE
DOING GOOD

Have a greater-than-you long-term goal

do
> *Verb*
> Gerund or present participle: doing
> - Have a specified effect on.
> "The walk will do me good".

Now, let's build on the "why" thinking I have outlined in the previous chapter.

Ultimately, the long-term beneficiary of your pursuit of mastery can be either your future self (e.g., "becoming an excellent actor / leader / musician…"), or something bigger than yourself (e.g., "helping others", "spreading joy in the world", "serving God", "serving the profession"). Most people have both a **self-oriented motive**, meaning that they want to get better and to make something out of themselves, and a **self-transcendent motive**, meaning that their getting better is in service of a bigger cause. For example, someone might want to get healthy to feel better (self-oriented motive) and to be around to help with the grandkids (self-transcendent motive); someone might want to become a car mechanic to have a job that matches her passion (self-oriented motive) and to make the most of her God-given talents (self-transcendent motive); someone might want to become a doctor to have a good career (self-oriented motive) and to help people heal (self-transcendent motive).

Regardless of whether they have a self-oriented motive or not, people who do have a self-transcendent motive for learning enjoy the following advantages: they learn better; they find more meaning in their pursuit of mastery; and they persist much more when the going gets tough. So whether it is a pro-social cause or a deity, having a self-transcendent perspective on your pursuit of mastery is a win-win: the outcome contributes to the greater good and the self-transcendent perspective helps you in the process.

For example, researchers carried out several studies involving about 2,000 high-school and college students, and reported their findings in a paper aptly titled: "Boring but important". It turns out that on average, compared with those who did not, students who had a self-transcendent purpose for learning achieved the following: they remained in school longer; had better grades; spent twice as much time reviewing tedious exam questions; and in one study, they solved about 35% more math problems during a computer session, even though the problems were boring and at any point in time they could switch to watching entertaining online videos.

Self-transcendent purpose beats YouTube® for high school and college students? That is pretty powerful stuff.

Now, before we get all excited, there is a caveat: having a self-transcendent purpose does not make learning activities fun. I am talking about activities such as practicing piano scales or performing algebra divisions again and again — they still feel boring. But people who have a self-transcendent purpose for learning persist longer, even though the task is tedious.

In other words, if you are serving a greater cause you are not going to quit when practice feels hard because you know that fun is not necessarily an attribute of serving.

The takeaway: who or what are you doing this for?

To learn more:
Grant, A. (2013). *Give and take: A revolutionary approach to success.* New York: Viking.

Yeager, D. S., Henderson, M. D., Paunesku, D., Walton, G. M., D'Mello, S., Spitzer, B. J., & Duckworth, A. L. (2014). Boring but important: A self-transcendent purpose for learning fosters academic self-regulation. *Journal of Personality and Social Psychology, 107*(4), 559-580.

Ingredients for Mastery

The 10 Ds for Mastery

CHAPTER SIX

DRILL

Deliberate practice

drill
> *Noun*
> - Instruction or training in military exercises.
> "Parade-ground drill".
> *Synonyms:* training, instruction, coaching, teaching, physical exercises, and workout.

In his bestseller: "Outliers: The story of success", Malcolm Gladwell popularized the "10,000 hours rule". In the words of the neurologist David Levitin who Malcom Gladwell quotes at length: "The emerging picture from such studies is that ten thousand hours of practice is required to achieve the level of mastery associated with being a world-class expert — in anything".

Well, it turns out that the picture is more complex than that. How much practice you need to achieve mastery depends on many factors, among which are the following: talent; personality; physical factors; age; and the kind of field chosen.

Moreover, 10,000 hours is an *average* value, the result of research led by Anders Ericsson on violin players at the Berlin's Academy of Music. In that foundational study, Ericsson and colleagues found that what sets apart potential soloist, the top of the top, from all other violin players was the amount of hours that they had been practicing: on *average* 10,000 hours.

Again, the key word is "average". Why?

Consider this. In another study, two psychologists studied a group of 104 competitive chess players. It turns out that it took the chess players on *average* 11,000 hours of practice to achieve master status (defined as accumulating 2,200 Elo points, according to the World Chess Federation's ranking system). So even more practice hours than what Ericsson found with violinists! However, instead of looking at the average, let's look at the range of values. One chess player got his master status after only 3,000 hours of practice, whereas it took another player 23,000 hours! That is roughly a difference of two decades! So, yes, 10,000 hours… on *average*.

Furthermore, deliberate practice is more relevant the more other factors are equal. For example, among NBA players deliberate practice matters a lot to separate champions from average players *precisely because other factors such as height, age, or arm to forearm ratio are pretty much the same*. By contrast, if you shoot hoops with friends during the weekend, it is very likely that everyone wants your six foot five friend on their team, deliberate practice or not.

Despite all these limitations, one thing is certain: **practice matters to achieve mastery**. Angela Duckworth, Professor of Psychology at the University of Pennsylvania and one of the foremost world experts on the psychology of achievement, came up with an interesting theory about mastery. According to Professor Duckworth and her co-authors, achievement is the product of talent and effort — with the latter winning in the long run. Her model is very elegant and is illustrated with Newtonian mechanics. But fear not: we won't have to brush up on Physics 101, we can use a metaphor to understand the idea. Here it goes: talent is the car you drive, and practice is the hours you drive. If you are very talented, it's as if you are driving a Ferrari. You are faster than pretty much anything else on the road. However, even a Ferrari can be outrun in the long run (sorry, could not resist the pun) by anyone willing to drive for more hours. So the old Toyota pick-up truck chugging along the freeway all night long will get to the destination sooner than the Ferrari whose driver stops to rest for the night.

So regardless of the level of talent you have, and regardless of the exact number of hours needed, putting in effort to practice is the key to achieving mastery.

But practice needs to be done right. It needs to be **deliberate practice**.

Deliberate practice has the following features:

a) It is *hard*. Be prepared. Even world-class performers cannot sustain it for more than a few hours each day.

b) It is focused on a *very specific aspect* of the performance. For example, if you are pursuing mastery in swimming, then a deliberate practice session might be only about the angle with which your hands impact the water when you swim freestyle. Or if you are learning German, a deliberate practice session might be specifically about pronouncing words with ü.

c) *Challenge must exceed skill*. Deliberate practice needs to push you out of your comfort zone. Deliberate practice focuses on weaknesses; it is not about rehearsing strengths.[1] Playing on the piano the sonata you know how to perform flawlessly is fun, but it is not practice. Practicing sections of the difficult sonata you do not yet know how to play is deliberate practice.

d) There should be feedback, *immediate feedback* if at all possible. In sports it is easy to do; for example, when you run a mile you can see your time immediately. That is your feedback. The same is true for musicians. When you play a piece, you hear it at the same time and you notice immediately if something is off. In other domains it is harder to get feedback, however it can be

---

[1] As Professor Angela Duckworth said in one of her presentations: "choose easy, work hard". In other words, choose what you want to master according to your strengths and interests (see the chapter "Direction") and then work on your weaknesses, i.e. the aspects of your performance that you need to improve the most.

done. For example, when studying a language, record yourself speaking in the foreign idiom and play back the recording immediately. When practicing delivering a presentation, videotape yourself and review the tapes immediately after each segment (e.g., opening, the first 30 seconds), and incorporate your own feedback right away by repeating the segment. Consider practicing with a buddy or hiring an experienced coach for this reason only (see the chapter "Detail").

e) *Repeat* until you achieve mastery of that specific aspect of the skill. In the example above of the piano sonata, you do not stop practicing it when you can perform it well enough once. You stop when you can perform it flawlessly 10 times in a row.

The takeaway: to achieve mastery, practice deliberately.

To learn more:
Campitelli, G., & Gobet, F. (2008). The role of practice in chess: A longitudinal study. *Learning and Individual Differences, 18*(4): 446–458.

Duckworth, A. L., Eichstaedt, J., & Unger, L. (2015). The mechanics of human achievement. *Social and Personality Psychology Compass, 9*(7), 359-369.

Ericsson, K. A., Krampe, R. T., & Tesch-Römer, C. (1993). The role of deliberate practice in the acquisition of expert performance. *Psychological Review, 100*(3), 363-406.

Gladwell, M. (2008). *Outliers: The story of success.* New York: Little, Brown and Company.

CHAPTER SEVEN
DETERMINATION

If... then... planning

de·ter·mi·na·tion
Noun
- Firmness of purpose; resoluteness.
"He advanced with an unflinching determination".
Synonyms: resolution, resolve, willpower, and strength of character.

The pursuit of mastery is a path where determination sets apart those who move forward from those who quit.

Determination is key when the going gets tough.
And it will, if you pursue new learning and if you are intent on developing new skills.

How can you get an extra boost of determination when you most need it?

A popular idea is that visualization can be a powerful motivating force.
According to this theory, to increase your motivation you should visualize the happy

ending: you performing at a master level, effortlessly.

That feels great. As matter of fact, it feels so great that the brain, tricked by the visualization, initiates a relaxation response, as if you actually reached the finishing line — tension goes away and the muscles relax.

Great strategy to calm your nerves, but not so great to mobilize your energy when, for example, you are still sweating at mile 2 and the finishing line is at mile 26.2. It's like switching off the engine mid-race.

However, there is a way to boost your motivation to act by using your imagination.

It requires a one-two Jedi mind trick.

Step one: first, what is a positive outcome of achieving your mastery goal, for example speaking Spanish fluently? You might think of something like the following: richer connection with the locals when traveling to Spain. Now imagine achieving your mastery goal, and let your mind savor the satisfaction of jabbering fluently in Spanish with cool Madrilenos as you sip sangria while enjoying the movida (= the night life).

That feels good — the speaking in Spanish, not the sangria.

But the visualization is only half of the process.

Back to reality, where your knowledge of Spanish hardly goes beyond "Gracias" and "Por Favor".

Ingredients for Mastery

Step two: Next, let's change gears. Think realistically about what can go wrong in your pursuit of mastering the Spanish language (for example, "I am tempted to go out with my friends instead of practicing"). Furthermore, and this is very important, think of what you can do about it (for example, "when my friends ask me to go out, I am going to say no").

Now just put them in *if... then...* format, and bam! You' ve got yourself an action plan: "If Mary and Johnny ask me to hang out with them, then I will tell them that I need to stay home to study Spanish".

Now repeat the process: step one again, step two again.

Remember step one is finding out a positive outcome of reaching your goal, and then visualizing it vividly; step two is thinking about what can go wrong in your pursuit of excellence (*if* this happens...) and thinking about how you can respond to that specific challenge (*then* I will do this...).

So in our example about speaking Spanish, another positive outcome could be the sense of pride you would feel in expressing yourself in a different language. You can bask in that for a few moments, but then again change gears and think of a potential obstacle, e.g., that at times practice might feel too hard. When that happens, you might resolve to remind yourself of how important it is to you, or you might resolve to think of a friend that you respect who managed to learn Spanish. In the latter case, your plan would be: "If practice feels hard, then I will remind myself of the fact that Mark did it."

The important thing to remember is that whereas visualization alone will relax you and zap your energy, this one-two mental move energizes you and feeds your determination.

Twenty-five years of research led by New York University Professor Gabriele Oettingen have shown that people using this strategy of contrasting wishes with obstacles do better in achieving goals in several different domains, such as the following: health (e.g., exercising more); school (e.g., achieving better grades); and relationships (e.g., being more self-confident).

The takeaway: the amateur imagines effortless success, the professional imagines success but expects and prepares for obstacles.

To learn more:

Duckworth, A. L., Kirby, T., Gollwitzer, A., & Oettingen, G. (2013). From fantasy to action: Mental contrasting with implementation intentions (MCII) improves academic performance in children. *Social Psychological and Personality Science, 4*(6), 745-753.

Oettingen, G. (2014). *Rethinking positive thinking: Inside the new science of motivation*. New York: Penguin.

CHAPTER EIGHT
DEDICATION

Grit

ded·i·ca·tion
Noun
- The quality of being dedicated or committed to a task or purpose.
"His dedication to his duties".
Synonyms: commitment, application, industry, resolve, enthusiasm, zeal, perseverance, persistence, tenacity, and staying power.

What separates top performers from good ones? According to the University of Pennsylvania Professor Angela Duckworth, the answer is grit, defined as **"passion and perseverance for long term goals"**. In fact, for most pursuits grit is a better predictor of success than measures of talent, such as IQ or SAT scores.

Grit separates aspiring US Army officers who survive the first weeks at West Point from those who do not: it is what distinguishes Spelling Bee finalists from other competitors; it is what separates highly rated teachers or top salespersons from the average ones.

We saw in the chapter "Drill" that to build the skills you need to succeed, you have to do deliberate practice; but deliberate practice is hard, and to sustain it you need grit: passion and perseverance.

You need **passion** to maintain a narrow focus on a subject for years upon years to achieve the mastery that can take you to the very top. Gritty people are obsessed by an idea or a field of endeavor, and make it their life pursuit. They live it and breathe it, day in and day out.

Because grit is about long-term goals, occasional lack of progress is inevitable — yet gritty people **persevere** until they get it done. No matter how many times they get knocked down, they always get up, dust themselves off and keep on going. They are the Edisons who try 1,000 times until the light bulb works.

It takes grit to achieve excellence.

If someone is not consistent in her interests, she might become good enough in different fields but excellent in none: she lacks the passion component of grit.

If someone is not persistent in pursuing his deep interests, he will quit when things get difficult or when months go by without any significant achievement or reward: he lacks the perseverance component of grit.

Grit is about running a marathon, not a sprint. It is about staying up each night an extra hour to study, month after month and year after year, not about pulling all-nighters the day before the test. Grit is about **stamina**, not intensity.

Dedication is different from discipline (see the related entry), just as **grit is different from self-control**. You can be very self-controlled and productive, but lacking a life-long passion you might jump from one career to another without achieving distinction in any. Or you can be very gritty about your field of work, yet lack self-control to resist temptations in other domains, such as food, impulse shopping, or sex. Tiger Woods, anyone?

Dedication is also different from stubbornness. Gritty people are dedicated to long-term pursuits, so their perseverance is at the strategic level, not at the tactical level: they keep their focus but they change and adapt their tactics as appropriate. In other words, a gritty person is committed to reaching a specific destination but remains open to re-evaluating and, if necessary, changing the way to get there; a stubborn person instead is committed not only to a destination but also to a specific route.

The take away: to achieve mastery, choose depth instead of breadth.

To learn more:
Duckworth, A.L., & Gross, J.J. (2014). Self-control and grit: Related but separable determinants of success. *Current Directions in Psychological Science, 23*(5), 319-325.

Duckworth, A. L., Kirby, T. A., Tsukayama, E., Berstein, H., & Ericsson, K. A. (2011). Deliberate practice spells success: Why grittier competitors triumph at the National Spelling Bee. *Social Psychological and Personality Science, 2*(2), 174-181.

Duckworth, A. L., Peterson, C., Matthews, M. D., & Kelly, D. R. (2007). Grit: Perseverance and passion for long-term goals. *Journal of Personality and Social Psychology, 92*(6), 1087-1101.

Duckworth, A. L., Quinn, P. D., & Seligman, M.E.P. (2009). Positive predictors of teacher effectiveness. *Journal of Positive Psychology, 19,* 540-547.

Keller, G., & Papasan, J. (2012). *The one thing: The surprisingly simple truth behind extraordinary results.* Austin, Texas: Bard Press.

CHAPTER NINE

DIGNITY

Perform (and fail) with dignity, self-respect and self-compassion

dig·ni·ty
   Noun
   - A sense of pride in oneself; self-respect.
   "It was beneath his dignity to shout".
   Synonyms: self-respect, pride, self-esteem, self-worth.

Learning new things is hard.
Running miles is hard.
Playing an instrument is hard.
Being a leader is hard.

Sometimes you might feel like complaining.

Sometimes you might be tempted to make a big show of your effort.

We all know "those ones" at the gym, who grunt and snort and mark each accomplished deadlift with shouts of triumph.

We all know "those ones" at the water cooler, always complaining about all the sacrifices they are making to attend to their freely chosen pursuits.

Don't be them.

This recommendation is based on my own personal bias towards the virtue of modesty.

It is also based on philosophy, namely Stoics' Ethics.

So feel free to take it or reject it.

There is, however, a scientific angle that supports my bias somewhat.

Containing yourself is an exercise in self-regulation, and as such it trains your willpower muscle (see the chapter "Discipline").

You will be stronger for it.

But how about times when we fail?

We might start the day with the best of intentions, for example with the following items on our to do list: going to the gym after work; no dessert at dinner; and writing for one hour after dinner.

Yet as night comes, to our surprise, we realize that not only we have managed to skip the gym and have some dessert after all; we've also made it well past bedtime without having written a single word because we have been binge watching the latest TV shows!

When we find ourselves in those situations, we have the opportunity to do something we are extremely good at: making excuses.

That is a way to restore the dignity that we feel we lost when we succumbed to temptation.

For example, suppose that I want to become excellent at the martial art Ju-Jitsu and that my goal is to hit the gym each evening after work. When I fail to do that, it is because:

- I had a rough day at work;
- Traffic was crazy and I got home 15 minutes later than usual;
- I felt tired;
- I deserved a break today;
- I did not sleep well last night;
- My work-out clothes are still in the laundry basket;
- My grappling buddy is not going to be at the gym today;
- It is raining and I do not feel like going to the gym;
- I really needed to talk to my friend;
- I was hungry and I had an early dinner;
- I needed to plan for my kid's birthday party;
- I had to start my tax filing;...

Here is the problem with excuses: they are true.
You did have a rough day at work.
You did feel tired.
It is raining.
And so on.

But guess what?
One excuse today, one excuse tomorrow, and your pursuit of excellence becomes just a figment of your imagination, in the same category as unicorns.

So what should we do?

1) **Calibrate your expectations: there is no perfect day.**

Accept the fact that very rarely will days unfold according to our plans.
Life gets in the way.
Make peace with that.
Problems will pop up.

2) **No excuses.**

Adopt a zero excuses policy. If you fail to do something, accept that.
You might have good reasons for failing to follow through, but do not turn those reasons into excuses.
Take full responsibility and move on; this is an act of self-respect.

3) **Self-compassion.**

Do not go from making excuses to flagellating yourself.
Instead, be compassionate towards yourself.
So you did not go to the gym. You failed this time. But that does not make you a bad person; it just makes you human. One misstep does not mean you will never excel (see chapter 13, "Delta"); it just means you need to plan better.
Accept your momentary lapse and show a little love to yourself: how would you treat a friend in the same situation? What would you tell

them if they called you to share how bad they feel because they did not go to the gym? What would a compassionate observer say?

4) **Lesson learned and next steps.**

On the other hand, research also shows that self-compassion alone without discipline to commit to do better can be an obstacle to achievement: there is the danger of indulging in self-compassion, feeling great but not achieving much.

So to get going, reflect on the following questions:

What did this day teach you?

How can you do better next time?

What can you do differently so that there is no next time (see the chapter "Dedication")?

To sum up, carry yourself with dignity in the pursuit of mastery.

When setbacks happen, and they will, don't make excuses for yourself and don't self-flagellate. Instead do the following: take ownership; practice self-compassion; plan better; and keep going.

The takeaway: in the pursuit of mastery, maintain your composure.

To learn more:

McGonigal, K. (2012). *The willpower instinct: How self-control works. Why it matters, and what you can do to get more of it.* New York: Penguin.

McNulty, J. K., & Fincham, F. D. (2012). Beyond positive psychology? Toward a contextual view of psychological processes and well-being. *American Psychologist, 67*(2), 101-110.

Neff, K. (2011). *Self-compassion: The proven power of being kind to yourself.* New York: HarperCollins.

Seneca, L.A. (1969). *Letters from a stoic.* London, England: Penguin.

CHAPTER TEN
DILIGENCE

Habits

dil·i·gence
> *Noun*
> - Careful and persistent work or effort.
>
> *Synonyms:* conscientiousness, assiduousness, assiduity, hard work, application, concentration, effort, care, industriousness, rigor, and meticulousness.

Diligence is showing up for your practice day in and day out, rain or shine.

But, wait, that requires a massive amount of self-control, right?

Actually no, it does not.

It turns out that people who are higher in self-control also report making less use of sheer willpower to resist temptations or to perform desired behaviors. How is that possible?

Enter habits.

People with high levels of self-control achieve their goals because they are methodical enough to establish a set routine to which they stick day after day. They are creatures of habits.

As Aristotle said more than two thousand years ago: "We are what we repeatedly do. Excellence then is not an act, but an habit".

Habits are nothing more and nothing less than connecting a cue (the trigger) with a specific behavior (the automatic desired response). For example, you sit down in the car (trigger), and automatically you wear the seatbelt (behavior). You see the red traffic light (trigger,) and automatically you hit the brakes (behavior). You approach the door to your house (trigger) and you turn off the alarm using the keychain remote (behavior). Even though afterwards you might realize that you never turned the alarm on in the first place — because it is the weekend and your family is home. Still you did it, automatically, without thinking. Out of habit.

That is the beauty of habits: no thinking required; no decisions to be made; and no need to involve willpower. Instead of engaging your brain in all those cognitive effortful activities, you can let it cruise on autopilot with the simple rule: when [trigger], then [practice].

This is good, because practice is hard enough without having to spend a lot of effort just to decide when and how to initiate it! It is no coincidence that studies report that about 50% of our daily behaviors are actually habits — from brushing your teeth to locking the door on your way out, from commuting home to turning on the TV for the 6 o'clock news.

PLANNING HABITS

So, how do you go about to establish the habit of daily practice?

By using the magic of the "if... then..." rule to create **instant habits** (see also the related chapter "Determination").

More specifically, you should have a plan that looks like this: If/when (trigger), then (behavior).

For example: "when it is 7 PM, then I will practice"; or "if I am alone in the house, then I will practice".

Any of the following can work as a trigger:
- A specific location (a room, a desk, a building) where you can practice;
- A specific time when you can practice;
- A specific emotional state (e.g., if bored, then I will review my notes);
- The presence or absence of specific people;
- One specific action that always precedes practice, e.g., getting out of bed, finishing dinner, or responding to emails. For example, you might have action plans such as "when I get out of bed, then I will put on my running gear"; or "immediately after finishing dinner, I will practice";
- Pre-scheduled reminders and alerts on your electronic devices.

Once you identify a suitable trigger, all you have to do is to connect it with the desired behavior. Remember, the formula is: when / if [trigger], then [practice].

ESTABLISHING HABITS

However, it takes time before "when/if… then…" combinations become true habits.

To make this habit-consolidation process easier, it is advisable to start very small. In fact, start with the smallest measurable step. Instead of "immediately after coming home from work, I will practice scales on the piano for one hour", go for "immediately after coming home from work, I will practice one scale". Instead of "when it is 6:30 AM I will go for a 30-minute run", go for "when it is 6:30 AM I will go for a three-minute run".

The key here is to have a "**no excuse**" resolution. You might find excuses for not going for a half-hour run, but not for skipping a three-minute run. You might find excuses for not listening to the whole German tape, but not for skipping listening for two minutes to the tape.

So to have a "no excuse" resolution, the "then…" part needs to be a micro-step.

Not only will you be more likely to engage in the desired behavior when the trigger happens (and that is your main goal); chances are that once you get started, you will keep going. Once you are out for a three-minute run, you might just as well run for another three; once you made the effort to sit at the piano to practice one scale, you might just as well practice two.

Ingredients for Mastery

Again: when you are establishing new habits, the key is to connect triggers with desired behaviors and to break through the inertia.

Once you start rolling, you are good.

Maintain the same cue over time, and adjust the difficulty of the behavior to practice as your proficiency increases (so, for example, the smallest step becomes a five-minute run, then a ten-minute run, then a thirty minute run and so forth).

MAINTAINING HABITS

Once you begin to practice automatically when the cue appears, you have made it — you have created the habit of diligently practicing.

Diligence, after all, is doing what you are supposed to do that day, each day, every day.

It is nothing less, but also nothing more.

So when the habit is established, it is time to switch gears.

To illustrate the idea of doing nothing less but also nothing more when it comes to sustain effort over time, here is a brief story, told by Jim Collins and Morten Hansen in their book "Great by choice": in 1911 two expeditions were racing to the South Pole. The British Royal Navy officer Robert Falcon Scott was leading one expedition, and the Norwegian Roald Amundsen was leading the other. Both were courageous men. Both made it to the South Pole. However, Amundsen got there first, bringing back home all of his team.

Scott got there second, and neither he nor any of his team returned — they perished of cold, starvation, and exhaustion on the way back. Historians credit Amundsen's success to his careful preparation. Moreover, Amundsen was very diligent: he and his team traveled between 15 and 20 miles each day, regardless of the weather. In bad days, when snowstorms hit and even traveling just 5 miles in a day was hard, they went for 15. In good days, when they could have traveled for 30 miles or more, they never exceeded 20. This is important: from a purely physical perspective, they never over-exerted themselves; from a psychological perspective, their actions proved who was in control: they set the pace, not the elements.

By contrast, Scott had his team rest on bad days, but push to exhaustion on good days. That strategy did not work.

Collins and Hansen argue that the ability to perform when conditions are rough and to hold back when conditions are good is one element that characterizes thriving companies and leaders.

Therefore, in the pursuit of mastery, show up every day for practice. As Woody Allen said, "showing up is 80% of success". To do this, make practice a habit. Once it becomes a habit, practice diligently doing what you are supposed to do for the day, nothing less but nothing more.

For example, if my training plan calls for a 5-mile run, I do just that.

If I am feeling low energy, I lower my pace, but still strive for 5 miles; if I am feeling in great shape, I stick to the 5 miles, and I do not go for 6 because I might get injured or get too tired to effectively practice the next day.

Here is another example: if I determine that I can coach up to three clients each day, that is what I shoot for.

If I only have two clients in my schedule and a third asks for a session, I gladly welcome him or her; but if a fourth prospect inquires, I decline. Even though it is a potential loss of income, I know I would not be at my best during the fourth session of the day.

The takeaway: to achieve mastery, make it a habit to practice daily within pre-set boundaries.

To learn more:

Arnold, C.L. (2014). *Small move, big change: Using microresolutions to transform your life permanently*. New York: Penguin.

Collins, J., & Hansen, M.T. (2011). *Great by choice: Uncertainty, chaos and luck — why some thrive despite them all*. New York: HarperCollins.

Duhigg, C. (2012). *The power of habit: Why we do what we do in life and business*. New York: Random House.

Galla, B.M. & Duckworth, A.L. (2015). More than resisting temptation: Beneficial habits mediate the relationship between self-control and positive life outcomes. *Journal of Personality and Social Psychology*. Advance online publication.

Ingredients for Mastery

CHAPTER ELEVEN
DISCIPLINE

The process model of self-control

dis·ci·pline
Noun
- The controlled behavior resulting from discipline.
"He was able to maintain discipline among his men".
Synonyms: control, training, teaching, regulation, order, authority, and rule.

It's hard to be disciplined in the pursuit of mastery.
Especially in this digital age, it is so difficult to get away from distractors — you have a world of entertainment at your fingertips, thanks to the Internet and social media.
Researchers found that the average time before a student turns to a distractor when doing homework is... 6 minutes!

However, new research also shows that we can outsmart temptations by building a multi-layered "defense system".

The military would call such a system the foundation for a "defense in depth" strategy.

You first fight temptations and distractions with the first line of defense, and if that is overrun, you fall back to the second line of defense, and so on.

What follows, then, is the list of our lines of defense built around our core intention to excel.

First line of defense: **choose your environment** — practice where there are no distractors. For example, if you need to study or to listen to language tapes, it is easier to do so at the library than at home; if you need to practice piano, it is easier to practice at Church than at home; and if you need to practice martial arts, it is easier to do that at the gym than in your home. Find and choose situations that enable the discipline required by your pursuit of excellence.

The environment also includes people; choose to hang out with the right kind of friends. For example, if you want to get better at running, hang out with other athletes; and if your practice demands that you get up early in the morning, hang out with people who go to bed early. Find and choose people that enable the discipline required by your pursuit of excellence.

Second line of defense: **modify your environment** to help you focus on practicing. Out of sight, out of mind. Design where you happen to be working on your craft so as to make practice easier and distraction harder. Depending on your pursuit, you can do any of the following: switch off the cellphone; turn off Wi-Fi on your computer; wear earplugs; get your running gear ready by the bed the night before a morning run;

keep your foreign language books handy and put the TV remote in a drawer in the kitchen. Again, the goal is to play to our laziness, making the desired behavior easier to perform and the counterproductive but tempting behaviors harder to perform. Even little tweaks help. For example, in a classic 2006 study, researchers at Cornell found that workers would eat twice as much candy if the treats were placed in a clear container (7.7 candies) than if they were in an opaque container (4.6 candies). In both cases the containers were on the workers' desks. Furthermore, when researchers moved the containers just six feet away, the number of candies eaten per day dropped in each condition, to 5.6 and 3.1 respectively. The difference between having the treats on your desk in a clear container and having them a few feet away in an opaque container amounts to 4.6 fewer candies per day. That adds up.

Third line of defense: **choose what you pay attention to**. Even in distracting environments, you can select what to focus on. Ignore the conversations around you, and focus on the book. Ignore the TV in the living room, and focus on your practice. Track the speaker at a conference instead of looking outside the window.

At the very least, be aware of what you are paying attention to. For example, if your pursuit of excellence involves writing, you might have to go online from time to time to look up things. But be on your guard, and pay attention to what you are doing. If you don't, that one-minute online fact check can easily morph into a twenty-minute mindless binge of social media feeds and YouTube videos.

Fourth line of defense: **mind tricks** to make distractions less tempting and deliberate practice more appealing.

Here are a few strategies:

- Use your imagination to reframe the situation. In your mind, the tempting dessert can become a blob of fat. Yours. Watching TV can be thought of as wasting time by staring at a glowing screen with your butt glued to a chair.

- Look at yourself from a third-party perspective. How would an observer describe what is going on? What if you were viewing the situation from the perspective of a fly on the wall or of an observer on a balcony? What would the observer say about your struggle with the distractor? Changing tacks, what would your mentor say if he or she was observing you now as you are dealing with this temptation?

- Bring your future self into the conversation. What would the future self say? How would your future self feel if he or she could not play the piano / speak a foreign language / be a good leader / be a marathon runner because you deemed cat videos more important than nurturing your practice?

Fifth and final line of defense; **just say no**.

If all of the above failed, use your willpower. Crush mind with mind. You can do it. Especially if you trained your willpower. That's right.

Evidence shows that you can train willpower as if it were just another muscle. Studies found that self-control can be enhanced by committing to small acts such as: improving your posture; cutting back on sweets; or using your non dominant hand to eat, to brush your teeth and to open doors. If you develop self-control in these tasks, then you increase the available willpower for when it really matters. Therefore, be creative; impose constraints, small ones, on what you do, just for the sake of exercising self-control. For example, go one month without a certain kind of food; or for six weeks resolve to park the car in the farthest spot in the parking lot, regardless of the weather or of how tired you are. Your willpower muscle will get stronger.

The takeaway: to maintain a disciplined effort in your pursuit of mastery, train your willpower and be smart in outsmarting distraction.

To learn more:
Ayduk, O., & Kross, E. (2010). From a distance: Implications of spontaneous self-distancing for adaptive self-reflection. *Journal of Personality and Social Psychology, 98*(5), 809-829.

Duckworth, A. L., Gendler, T. S., & Gross, J. J. (2014). Self-control in school-age children. *Educational Psychologist, 49*(3), 199-217.

Duckworth, A.L., Gendler, T.S., & Gross, J.J. (2016). Situational strategies for self-control.

Perspectives on Psychological Science, 11(1), 35-55.

McGonigal, K. (2012). *The willpower instinct: How self-control works. Why it matters, and what you can do to get more of it.* New York: Penguin.

Rosen, L. D., Carrier, L. M., & Cheever, N. A. (2013). Facebook and texting made me do it: Media-induced task-switching while studying. *Computers in Human Behavior, 29*(3), 948-958.

Wansink, B., Painter, J. E., & Lee, Y. K. (2006). The office candy dish: Proximity's influence on estimated and actual consumption. *International Journal of Obesity,* 30, 871–875.

White, R. E., Kross, E., & Duckworth, A. L. (2015). Spontaneous self-distancing and adaptive self-reflection across adolescence. *Child Development, 86*(4), 1272–1281.

CHAPTER TWELVE

DRIVE

Optimism, power poses and progress-focus

drive
Noun
A vigorous onset or onward course toward a goal or objective.
"The drive toward the goal line".
Synonyms: ambition, eagerness, attack, vigor, and energy.

To achieve mastery, you need drive. You need to have energy, enthusiasm, vigor and zest. It is fuel to your pursuit of excellence.

One psychological characteristic will be extremely useful to sustain your drive: **optimism**. The fun thing is that optimism can be learned.

Psychologists talk about optimism in at least two different ways:
1) As the expectation that things will turn out for the best. This is probably what most people mean when they call themselves optimists. Clearly, this perspective helps. Why start anything if you do not believe you will succeed, in the end?

2) As a way in which we make sense of events, both successes and failures (what psychologists call an "explanatory style"). We will focus on this perspective because there are some well-tested ways to develop optimism as an explanatory style.

How does optimism work as a way to make sense of events, then?

Suppose that you are learning Japanese; one day, as you stroll down the street, a tourist from Japan asks for information in broken English. Great, a chance to show off your skills! You answer the tourist's query in Japanese, and a brief conversation ensues. Until at some point it is clear that you cannot understand each other. You have to go back to English.

Let's listen in on how pessimists and optimists explain to themselves what just happened.

Pessimist: "Of course I totally screwed up. I am bad at learning languages, what did I expect? I was never good at it and never will be. I am a disaster, I will never learn Japanese."

Optimist: "Well, it went well up to a certain point, but then he lost me because I do not have such a wide vocabulary yet. I was not ready for such a difficult conversation right after lunch, without my notes! That poor dude clearly overestimated my proficiency in Japanese because he used fancy words! I will do better next time."

So pessimists take this brief conversation and explain it the following way: the bad outcome is permanent ("I was never good at learning languages and never will be"); the bad outcome means that they are personally flawed ("I am a disaster"); and the bad outcome is 100% their fault ("I totally screwed up").

By contrast, optimists take bad outcomes and explain them in terms that are temporary ("I was not ready for such a difficult conversation right after lunch, without my notes"), specific to the event ("I do not have such a wide vocabulary yet"), and external ("he overestimated my proficiency in Japanese"; blame for the negative outcome is shared).

Who do you think is more likely to persist in learning Japanese?

So, as you get ready to unleash yourself on the path to excellence, make sure to master an optimist's explanatory style. It is just as correct a viewpoint as the pessimist's one, and it can boost your drive to excel.

Not so big on working on the mind? Fear not, the body is another pathway to nourish your drive.

Psychologists have been investigating the effects of our posture and of how we carry ourselves. They found that adopting a "**power pose**" increases feelings of power, reduces anxiety, and enhances feelings of physical strength. More importantly for us, adopting a power pose also leads to an increase in self-confidence, optimism, and the likelihood of taking action.

So how do you adopt a power pose? Simply by taking up space with your body, for one to two minutes top, in an open posture.

For example, stand up, plant your feet firmly on the ground perpendicular to your shoulders and place your hands on your hips. Open up your chest and look straight ahead, with your chin up. This is the "wonder woman" pose.

Or, if you are sitting at a desk, push your chair back, cross your feet on the desk and put your hands behind your neck, taking up as much space as possible.

Obviously you do this when you are alone, before practice or as a break during practice.

Adopting power poses such as these every once in a while can contribute to sustaining your drive.

Another thing that can help you replenish your drive is **focusing on progress**.

The Harvard Professor Teresa Amabile and colleagues found in their research that the key to motivation is the sense that you are making progress, however small, in work that you deem meaningful (yet another reason to choose to master something that matters to you, as I argued in chapter one).

As someone who has overcome many running injuries over time, I can attest to this. What kept me going during long months of rehab was the little progress I was making, week after week.

So in your pursuit of mastery, focus on small progress.

When reflecting on your practice, do not think about what you are not yet capable of doing. Focus instead on the little things that you managed to accomplish this week compared to the week before.

The focus on small progress will maintain your drive during rough patches, and it will push you into over-drive when things are flowing smoothly!

The takeaway: nourish your drive to achieve mastery by adopting an optimistic explanatory style, by using power poses, and by focusing on progress.

To learn more:

Amabile, T., & Kramer, S. (2011). *The progress principle: Using small wins to ignite joy, engagement, and creativity at work.* Boston, MA: Harvard Business Review Press.

Carver, C. S., Scheier, M. F., Miller, C. J., & Fulford, D. (2009). Optimism. In S. J. Lopez & C. R. Snyder (Eds.), *Oxford Handbook of Positive Psychology* (pp. 303-311). New York: Oxford University Press, Inc.

Cuddy, A. (2015). *Presence: Bringing your boldest self to your biggest challenges.* New York: Little, Brown & Company.

Seligman, S. (1990). *Learned optimism: How to change your mind and your life.* New York: Random House.

How to Achieve Excellence Using Positive Psychology

CHAPTER THIRTEEN
DELTA

Growth mindset

del·ta
Noun
MATHEMATICS
- Variation of a variable or function.

On TV or on the Internet you can watch performers do amazing things, clearly mastering their craft: the virtuoso pianist; the amazing basketball player; and the flawless inspirational speaker.

Sometimes you can find those examples of excellent performance closer to home: your neighbor achieving a new personal record in a marathon; your friend mastering a foreign language; and your colleague bagging more sales.

The gap between what you can do and what they achieve seems unbridgeable: you can barely wrap your mind around the basics, and they are demonstrating flawless mastery.

But here is what you do not see: the countless hours of practice; the sweat and tears of the daily grind to get better; and the endless repetitions of the different skill sets required to achieve mastery.

You see the finished product, not the work that went into it. Money does not grow on trees; you need to work to make money. Similarly, masterful performance is not a fruit that can just be picked ripe and ready; it needs to be nurtured. It needs to grow.

No one is born anything. Even if you are a "math person", were you actually born knowing how to do algebra? No, you learned it. You needed to invest effort to become proficient at math.

Effort is good.
But to appreciate that, you need to have a growth mindset.

Carol Dweck earned her place in the pantheon of famous psychologists thanks to her work on the growth mindset. The Stanford Professor has been finding out in her studies that people view ability in two very different ways: either as fixed or as something that can grow.

The former is a **fixed mindset**. Whatever the ability, you believe that you either have "it" or not. You are either a smart person or not. You are either a people person or not. You are either a math person or not. From the fixed mindset perspective, achievement proves that you are smart and talented, whereas effort proves that you are not cut for it.

The opposite is a **growth mindset**. Whatever the ability, you believe that it is something that you can grow and improve. You believe that you can get smarter; or that you can get better in social interactions; or that you can improve your math skills. From a growth mindset perspective, it is not about proving yourself but it is about getting better; effort is good because it is a sign that you are learning new things.

For example, suppose Mark wants to master the art of Zen meditation.

Mark has been interested for a while about Eastern philosophies, and he has read a lot about the benefits of meditation; he really wants to learn meditation and he is fully committed.

Mark gives it a try and it seems that nothing is happening, other than him spending several minutes a day staring at a white wall and expending a lot of effort trying to sit still. Thinking of his neighbor who tells him about spending 30 minutes a day meditating, and how she wishes she could do more, Mark starts thinking that maybe he is not cut out for this kind of discipline. Mark ends up blaming Auntie Elda for passing on to him a "monkey mind", and he concludes that meditation is not for him. He thinks that he lacks the magic "meditation ability". Mark has a fixed mindset.

Now consider this alternative scenario with the same premises.

Mark starts meditating and it seems as if nothing is happening, other than him spending several minutes a day staring at a white wall and expending a lot of effort trying to sit still. Thinking of his neighbor who tells him about spending 30 minutes a day meditating, and how she wishes she could do more, Mark thinks that he needs to do more. He thinks that the fact that he is spending all this effort means that he has a "monkey mind" to conquer, a worthy challenge. The benefits of mastering meditation will be huge, and so Mark resolves to stick with it. From this perspective, effort is good and it is a sign that he is stretching himself to learn something new. Mark has a growth mindset.

People with a fixed mindset see failure and effort as signs that they do not have the right stuff. Failure is a judgment on their worth.
People with a growth mindset see failure and effort as signs that they are growing. Failure is just feedback that can be used to do better next time.
Mindsets are a choice. Choose to believe that you can grow, learn, and develop your skills. Choose to believe that effort is good.

The takeaway: the delta between where you are and where you want to be in your pursuit of mastery simply means that you are not there... <u>yet</u>.

To learn more:
Dweck, C. (2006). *Mindset: The new psychology of success*. New York: Random House.

CHAPTER FOURTEEN

DOWNTIME

The art of maintenance

down·time
   Noun
   NORTH AMERICAN
   - A time of reduced activity or inactivity.
   "Everyone needs downtime to unwind".
   Synonyms: free time, spare time, break, rest, and respite.

Don't forget to recharge your batteries.

Deep work and deliberate practice require time for your body and for your mind to absorb the learning; moreover, you want to show up full of energy for the next practice session, right?

What constitutes recovery from deliberate practice depends very much on the kind of activity, so the general recommendation is as follows: **eat right**; **move** any chance you get (unless your mastery pursuit involves some kind of physical activity); and get enough **sleep**.

Therefore:

- Experiment and figure out which foods give you the most energy and which foods are healthier for you.

- Have a regular workout routine, and walk whenever you can: during lunch break; by parking the car in the farthest spot of the parking lot; by taking the stairs instead of the elevator.

If you spend a lot of time in front of a computer, consider setting up a stand up desk. If you are more adventurous, consider setting up your laptop on an old treadmill and walk at a slow pace as you use the computer. It might take awhile to get used to it, but it pays off.

- Figure out how many hours of sleep you need, and stick with that number, whatever it might be: 7, 8 or 9.

I know, sometimes finding time for a good night's sleep can be a challenge.

But before accepting chronic lack of sleep, get rid of late night wasted time: the mindless internet surfing or TV watching when you are too tired to do anything else, including going to sleep.

Set a **rhythm** for your practice.

For example, alternate 45 minutes of deep work (no distraction and intense focus) with 15 minutes of rest; or something similar, depending on the kind of practice.

The point here is that rest allows for springs of focused efforts.

Just make sure that rest is actual rest.

If your practice requires sitting at a desk in front of a computer, then opening your Facebook page or watching a YouTube video does not qualify as rest!

Instead, get up, stretch, do push ups, strike a yoga pose, step out, or talk to someone — to a real person, not to an avatar on your screen.

On the other hand, if your practice requires movement, then do the opposite: sit down, read something, engage your brain, talk to someone, and let your body rest.

Now, take this idea of rhythm and scale it up to **your life**, as you are engaged in a meaningful pursuit.

Chances are that you are missing a beat: one of the dangers of dedication to a craft is that we might get self-absorbed to the point of selfishness.

How do we deal with this problem?

First of all, I hope that your pursuit of excellence takes place in the context of a pro-social ultimate goal (see the chapter "Doing good").

Second, researchers find that problems arise not when there is too much dedication or grit per se; rather, problems arise when dedication or grit are neither balanced nor tempered by other factors, such as kindness, gratitude or humility.

To borrow a metaphor from Schwartz and Sharpe (2006), the latter situation would be analogous to that of a body builder who only works on his chest and arms and ignores all the rest until he can barely stand up. There is nothing wrong with massive arms and chest, if they are supported by a strong core and legs.

The topic of how we can cultivate a balanced character goes well beyond the scope of this little book.

Suffice it to say that while you are relentlessly pursuing excellence, you should also remember to work your other-oriented strengths and virtues such as kindness; love; compassion; gratitude; and to make things lighter on everybody, humor.

The takeaway: to achieve excellence, you also need to master the art of how to take care of yourself and others.

To learn more:

Rath, T. (2015). *Are you fully charged? The 3 keys to energizing your work and life.* Siliconguild.

Schwartz, B., & Sharpe, K. E. (2006). Practical wisdom: Aristotle meets positive psychology. *Journal of Happiness Studies, 7*(3), 377-395.

CHAPTER FIFTEEN
DETAIL

Team power

de·tail
> *Noun*
> - A small detachment of troops or police officers given a special duty.
> "The candidate's security detail".
> *Synonyms:* unit, detachment, squad, troop, contingent, outfit, and task force.

Details (in the sense of small differences) are key in deliberate practice.

But here I want to evoke another meaning of detail, as you see in the definition provided above: that of a group of people who have the same task.

Create a mission-focused detail. Create or seek out a **tribe** of friends engaged in the pursuit of mastery, even if in different fields. The group will provide you with support, encouragement, and accountability. That is why we have AA group meetings, fellowships in Church, or SEAL teams.

We are gritty with others and for others.

Moreover, recent research shows that emotions and behaviors are contagious: it matters who your friends are. That applies to the bad things (e.g., when a person gains weight, close friends tend to gain weight too), and to the good things (e.g., if you surround yourself with happy people, it is likely you will become happier).

It is reasonable to think that this same contagion effect applies to grit, engagement and the pursuit of mastery.

If you want to take it one step further and go pro, hire a **coach**.

Coaches are essential for developing and maintaining mastery.

A good coach can break down the mechanics of the behaviors that you need to perform flawlessly to achieve mastery. A great coach can give you immediate and accurate feedback, therefore playing an essential role in helping you practice in a deliberate way (see the chapter "Drill"). An excellent coach knows when to use positive feedback to get you going, and when to use negative feedback to perfect your performance.

If hiring a coach is too much, then at a minimum enlist someone (a friend, your spouse, or a family member) whose job is to not let you quit on a bad day. Do this because there are going to be bad days, and we cannot always be strong. Sometimes, someone else needs to be strong for us.

The takeaway: travel the path to mastery with like-minded friends. Consider hiring a coach.

To learn more:
Christakis, N. A., & Fowler, J. H. (2007). The spread of obesity in a large social network over 32 years. *New England Journal of Medicine, 357*(4), 370-379.

Fowler, J. H., & Christakis, N. A. (2008). Dynamic spread of happiness in a large social network: Longitudinal analysis over 20 years in the Framingham Heart Study. *BMJ: British Medical Journal, 337*.

Gawande, A. (2011). Personal best: Top athletes and singers have coaches. Should you? *New Yorker Magazine*. Retrieved from: http://www.newyorker.com/magazine/2011/10/03/personal-best.

Ingredients for Mastery

Through duty to delight

CHAPTER SIXTEEN
DELIGHT

Flow

de·light
 Noun
 Great pleasure.
 "She took great delight in telling your story".
 Synonyms: pleasure, happiness joy, glee, gladness.

The path to mastery is hard: drill; determination; dedication; diligence; and discipline.

Yet if we stick to it, we can experience delight, or, more accurately, flow.

Flow is being "in the zone". Flow is when you are totally absorbed in the task at hand, so much so that the self disappears, and time flies. Hours feel like seconds. You become one with your performance, which flows (it seems) effortlessly and with no conscious direction. Instead of you being in control, you are just a tool of the performance unfolding through you.

Flow is awe inspiring to witness: Keith Jarrett at the 1975 Köln Concert; Michael Jordan in the zone; Tony Robbins leading one of his workshops; and so on and so forth.

According to the University of Pennsylvania Professor Martin Seligman, flow is one of the main routes to authentic happiness.

Flow occurs when there is the right balance between skill and challenge — when what you are practicing is difficult enough for your skill level, but not too difficult.

However, you need to first dutifully undergo the grind of deliberate practice before experiencing the delight of flow.

The psychologist Mihaly Csikszentmihaly, who first conceptualized the idea of flow, noted that **skilled performance** is a necessary condition for flow to occur. But guess what you need to do to develop skilled performance? That's right, back to drill; determination; dedication; diligence; and discipline.

Once you reach a certain level of skill, the effortless flow emerges from the effortful practice in a mutually reinforcing expression of excellence. Duty and delight nourish each other.

The takeaway: stick with it long enough, and flow will provide all the motivation you need in the pursuit and expression of mastery.

To learn more:
Csikszentmihaly, M. (1990). *Flow: The psychology of optimal experience.* New York: HarperCollins.

Seligman, M. (2002). *Authentic happiness: Using the new positive psychology to realize your potential for lasting fulfillment.* New York: Free Press.

Von Culin, K. R., Tsukayama, E., & Duckworth, A. L. (2014). Unpacking grit: Motivational correlates of perseverance and passion for long-term goals. *The Journal of Positive Psychology, 9*(4), 306-312.

Dr. Paolo Terni, MAPP

Dr. Paolo Terni is originally from Italy, and he now lives and works in California.

In his life, Paolo has applied the principles outlined in this book to achieve excellence in many pursuits, ranging from mastery of the English language (677/677 in the Test of English as a Foreign Language, 1996) to excellence in the art of coaching (ICF Professionally Certified Coach); from running marathons to achieving two graduate degrees with honors (Doctor in Philosophy, 1994; Master in Applied Positive Psychology, 2014) in two different continents (State University of Milan, Italy; University of Pennsylvania, Philadelphia, USA).

Paolo works as an educator and has been facilitating workshops and coaching leaders since 1997. Organizations, executives and professionals hire Paolo when they need to achieve sustainable change in a short time; when they want to achieve excellence; and when they want to leverage their strengths and values to create their own signature leadership style.

Always eager to learn, Paolo is currently involved in research projects and pro-bono work focusing on character development and mindsets that promote achievement. A published author, Paolo's writings range from peer reviewed articles to children's books.

To hire Paolo to coach you on how to apply the strategies presented in this book to your life, or to coach you on how to achieve sustainable change in just a few sessions, send an email to: *briefcoachingsolutions at gmail.com* or visit his website at: www.briefcoachingsolutions.com.

www.ingramcontent.com/pod-product-compliance
Lightning Source LLC
Chambersburg PA
CBHW071315040426
42444CB00009B/2023